*This book honors the whole child and the child within, both young and old.
To my boy, we call "Seven" you make me shine son; I am honored and
privileged to be your mom. I love you. Thank you for choosing me.
To Hayden, you are your mommy's precious gem.*

*To Dr. Michael Bernard Beckwith, I am in deep gratitude for all the years of
continued unconditional love, and for the Life Visioning Process principles.
You have always stayed with me, I love you.
Dr. Brandi Jackson, thank you for your generosity.*

*When we empower children to become rooted and self-actualized
we allow them to feel, think, and believe the truth of who they are.
This book is for all of them- those beautiful souls that shine.*

Spirit

Library of Congress Control Number: 2013904316

ISBN: 978-0-615-74928-0
Spirit's Jewels
spirit@spiritsjewels.com
www.spiritsjewelsbooks.com

Printed in the United States of America

JEWELS
and the
Treasure ME
Discovery

Jewels bolted through the backdoor
and jumped off the porch in one
huge gigantic leap.

Running as fast as she could,
Jewels made a super dash through the
backyard with a huge smile on her face...

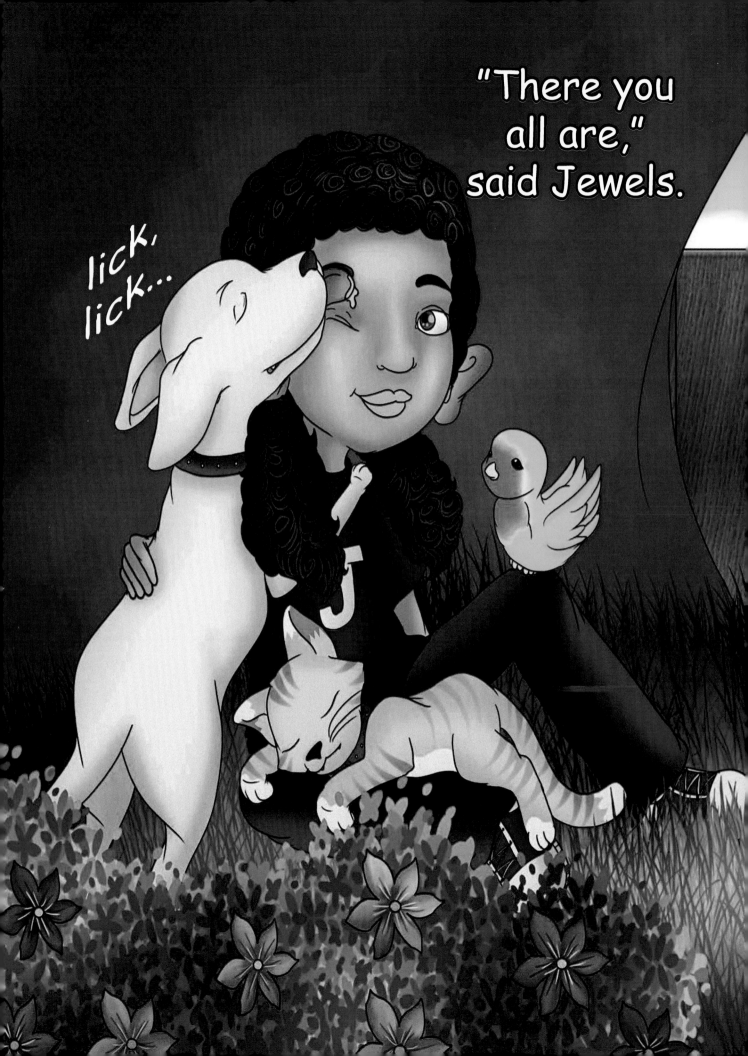

Jewels had such unconditional love
for each of her animals...

Bijou the lovebird, her tabby cat Amethyst,
and lovable yellow lab, Baby Gem.

Jewels wondered how other
kids saw themselves?
"Do they like who they are," she thought?

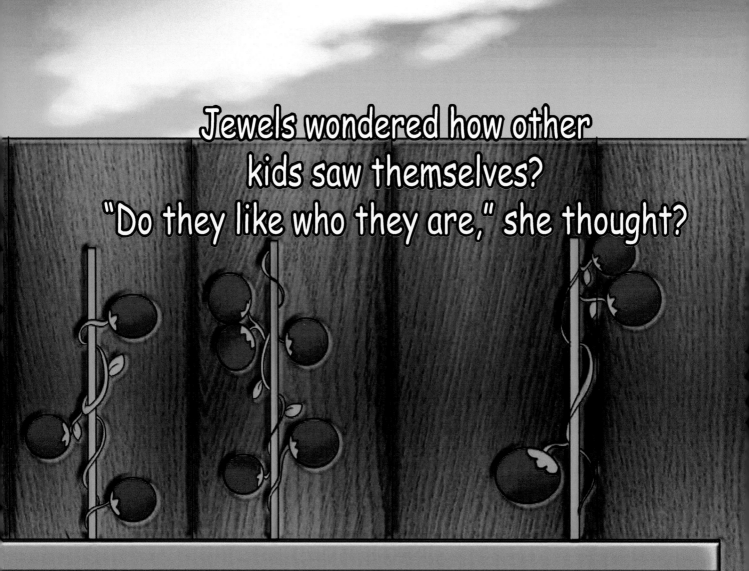

"We are all important, and we are all special!"

Jewels believed
she was important and special...
and she believed that for
other children too!

Jewels thought a lot
while swinging...

"I feel good about me,
and I have lots of fun!"

"Baby Gem always feels good,
her licks of love show me she does...
and she has lots of fun too!"

"We have great energy together,"
said Jewels to herself.

Jewels, was a big thinker
with a huge imagination...

she always saw possibility...

Jewels loved to play and discover
even on her own.

"Okay," shouted Jewels using her
outside voice...

"I think I know what we are
going to do today..."

You could hear Jewels laughing
as her ponytails flipped and flopped
in the wind.

Jewels shouted as they ran...

"We are going on an adventure...
A treasury discovery!"

Everywhere Jewels looked she found more colorful stones, with special messages on each of them.

By the end of the day Jewels had
a bag full of beautiful stones.

Each stone reminded Jewels of
who she was with a positive message.

That night while in bed
Jewels made a necklace.

Jewels knew she would
treasure each piece,
and each lesson discovery.

"A string of treasure
to last forever,"
Jewels said
to herself.

Jewels loved the adventure,
and the
Treasure ME Discovery!

Jewels prayed that night...

"Thank you for making me special,
and thank you for making me, ME!"

Kid Jemz...

How does Jewels feel about her animals?

How does Jewels feel about herself?

What did Jewels learn on her treasury discovery?

Do you think Jewels is a happy and fun kid?

How do you show your happiness?

Do you love you, for you?

Say something good about YOU!
Begin with I AM...

You are perfect, whole, and complete!